Daniel Boone

FRONTIER ADVENTURES

by Keith Brandt
illustrated by John Lawn

Troll Associates

Library of Congress Cataloging in Publication Data

Brandt, Keith (date)
    Daniel Boone, frontier adventures.

    Summary: Traces the boyhood years of the celebrated
frontiersman who, as a Quaker in Pennsylvania, learned
the skills which would make him the leader in opening
up the Wilderness Road to Kentucky.
    1. Boone, Daniel, 1734-1820—Juvenile literature.
2. Frontier and pioneer life—Kentucky—Juvenile
literature.   3. Pioneers—Kentucky—Biography—Juvenile
literature.   4. Kentucky—Biography—Juvenile
literature.   [1. Boone, Daniel, 1734-1820.   2. Pioneers.
3. Frontier and pioneer life]   I. Lawn, John, ill.
II. Title.
F454.B7295   1983   976.9'02'0924   [B]   [92]   82-15915
ISBN 0-89375-843-4
ISBN 0-89375-844-2 (pbk.)

Daniel Boone

FRONTIER ADVENTURES

Daniel Boone

FRONTIER ADVENTURES

Some people like to stay in one place all their lives. They dislike change. They are afraid of new things, and of being different from everyone around them. For them, the old ways are always the best.

Other people love the challenge of new things and new places. They follow their own beliefs, even if it's the unpopular thing to do. George and Mary Boone were like this.

Leaving England for the American colonies in the early 1700s was a huge challenge. But that didn't stop the Boones and their nine children from making the dangerous ocean crossing. They were looking forward to their new life in Pennsylvania. They had heard that the land there was cheap, plentiful, and produced fine crops. It was said that the woods were filled with wild game. The Boones knew that life on the frontier would not be easy. But they also believed that anyone willing to work hard could live a good life in this bountiful new land.

The Boones also looked forward to practicing their religion freely. They were Quakers. In England, Quakers were treated harshly for their beliefs. There would be none of that in Pennsylvania.

Soon after landing in the colonies, the family traveled to Oley Township. Oley, about fifty miles west of Philadelphia, was a new settlement at the edge of the wilderness. There, George Boone built a sturdy log cabin for his family. He

cleared many of his four hundred acres of land for farming. Soon he was a leading citizen in the colony. He founded the Oley Meeting House for the local Quaker community. And he became a justice of the peace.

A hard-working, fair, and honorable man, George was well respected in Oley. So were all of his children, especially his second son, Squire.

As a teenager, Squire Boone learned two trades. He was both a weaver and a blacksmith. At first, he worked for other people. Then, after he married Sarah Morgan and they began a family, Squire settled on his own farm in Oley. It was there, on November 2, 1734, that Daniel

Boone was born. He was the sixth of eleven children born to Sarah and Squire.

Before he was a year old, Daniel was walking— and running, too. He could never stay still for long. It wasn't a real problem at home, where there was plenty of space for roaming. Little Daniel could wander through the corn field, into the woods right behind the house, or down to the shallow stream, and always be safe.

But Daniel didn't wander only at home. Once a month, the local Quakers held services at their Meeting House. A meeting often lasted for hours. This was fine for all the Boones—except Daniel. Sitting still for more than five minutes at a time was torture for him. Mrs. Boone had to hold his hand firmly every moment. If she let go, he would slip away and disappear.

Daniel's vanishing act became a family joke. His older brother, Israel, once said, "Daniel is like chimney smoke on a windy day. Even as you look at it, it is gone."

Mr. and Mrs. Boone never worried much about little Daniel's wanderings. He had a wonderful sense of direction. Even if he went deep into the woods, he'd be sure to find his way home before supper. It was as if he had been born with a magical gift of never getting lost.

Daniel was an easy child to raise—as long as he wasn't asked to stay indoors. He was bright and good-tempered and strong and not at all lazy. He enjoyed doing any chore that took him outside.

One of the things he liked to do most was help his father in their small forge barn. Mr. Boone was a fine blacksmith, and his forge was his most important tool. In it blazed the fire used to heat and shape metal objects. Mr. Boone made nails, hammer-heads, axe-heads, and other things out

of iron. Some of these were for himself. Others he sold or traded to neighbors for things the Boones needed. Daniel's first job at the forge was pumping the big bellows. This fed air to the fire, keeping it roaring while his father worked.

When Daniel was seven years old, Mr. Boone showed him how to make iron nails. He took a piece of iron, softened it in the fire, and hammered it into a long, thin rod. Next, he hammered one end to a point. After that, he cut off a piece a few inches long at the pointed end of the rod. This piece was heated in the red-hot forge.

When the piece of iron was very hot, it was put into a nail-header. This was a thick wooden paddle with a hole in one end. The hole was just big enough to let most of the nail pass through. But the thickest part of the nail stuck out of the nail-header. Then a heavy hammer was used to pound the thick end until it was flat. Now the Boones had a nail with a sharp point and a broad, flat head.

Mr. Boone could make hundreds of nails a day. Young Daniel couldn't match that, but it wasn't long before he was turning out fifty to sixty a day. Daniel was very proud of his new skill, and so was his father.

Young Daniel learned to do a lot of things on the Boone farm. He learned to plant corn and vegetables, to plow the fields, and to harvest the crops. He could cut hay and stack it into neat piles called hay ricks. He knew how to fell trees and chop them into firewood, and how to split logs into boards, build a cabin, and make furniture.

Daniel also learned to tend the farm animals. And he could make tools, dig a well, and repair anything inside and outside the house. He learned to clean and fix a rifle. And to make and set traps for catching wild animals. His father believed a frontier boy should learn every skill he could, and Daniel was a very happy—and able— learner.

All of these skills would be useful to Daniel when he grew older. As a frontiersman, he would spend most of his time far from towns and people. He always settled miles away from anyone else, out where he had to do everything for himself. And when others began to settle nearby, he would pack up his family and move on. The need to go roaming never left him.

Young Daniel learned to take care of himself in other ways. As a Quaker, he was taught to keep out of fights and arguments, if possible. He didn't like to fight. He did like to swim, to run, and to wrestle with his cousins and friends. He spent a lot of free time with his best friends, Henry Miller and Abraham Lincoln (who would be remembered as the grandfather of President Abraham Lincoln).

What the boys enjoyed doing most was going into the woods with their bows and arrows. In those days, it was important to know how to shoot straight—to have a steady hand and a keen eye. Boys learned to use a rifle while they were still young, but only when they were with a father, uncle, or older brother. Until they were at least eleven or twelve, the only shooting they did on their own was with a bow and arrow.

Daniel and his friends held many archery contests. One day the target might be a thick oak tree, fifty yards away. Another day they might aim at a slim birch sapling, thirty yards away. Sometimes they tossed a corncob into the air and tried to shoot an arrow into it.

Most people missed targets like that. Not Daniel. He had a natural talent for shooting, and he could hit two out of every three corncobs thrown. When it came to target shooting with a bow and arrow, Daniel Boone was the best in his part of the country.

The boys also used their bows and arrows for hunting. The woods were full of rabbits, squirrels, quail, turkeys, and other wild game. Anything the boys brought down with an arrow was taken home for dinner. And Daniel, who was able to glide through the trees and shrubs in silence, always managed to bring back something for the dinner table.

Whenever Daniel went into the woods, he tried to think of himself as an Indian. For as long as Daniel could remember, he had admired Indians. They hunted better than any settler he knew. They could make a fire without using flint or steel. They knew which wild plants were safe to eat, and which ones to use as medicine. And they loved the wilderness, the way he did.

The Shawnee and Delaware Indians in the area all came to know and like the Boone boy. He was not like most of the other settlers. He treated them with respect. He asked them questions all the time, listened carefully to everything they said, and was very happy to learn from them. Because of this, they were willing to answer his questions and to teach him the ways of the forest.

The Indians taught Daniel to walk through the woods as they did, without leaving a trace. They taught him to move as swiftly and quietly as they did, so that even the animals would not know he was near. They taught him to follow the almost invisible trail left by deer traveling through the woods.

They also taught Daniel how to hide downwind at a pond. This way, the animals coming to drink would not see or smell him. The young frontier boy especially liked being "invisible" this way. It was thrilling to watch the deer, buffalo, and bears as close as five feet from his hiding place—and know they did not have any idea that he was there.

When Daniel was ten, the Boones bought twenty-five acres of pasture land. It was four miles away from their farm, and had the richest grass in that part of Pennsylvania. Grazing on this grass, their cows would grow fat and give plenty of milk. Mr. Boone planned to use most of the milk for making butter and cheese. These he would sell at a good profit.

There was just one problem—the four miles between the pasture and the farm. If the cows were taken from the farm every morning and walked back from the pasture every night, they wouldn't get fat enough and give as much good milk. The answer was to keep the cows on the pasture all summer. This meant that someone had to live out there to tend the cows.

Mr. Boone built a one-room cabin at the edge of the pasture. Then Mrs. Boone and Daniel moved in for the summer. Every morning, at sunrise, Daniel would turn the cows loose. They would graze contentedly all day. At sundown, the boy's job was to round up the herd and bring them to the cabin for milking.

Every day, Mrs. Boone churned the milk into butter and cheese, and wrapped them in cloth. Then Daniel took the wrapped food down to the spring behind the cabin. There, he put it into the water, which was ice cold and kept the food from spoiling. At week's end, two of Daniel's brothers, Samuel and Jonathan, rode out from the farm. They brought family news, local gossip, fruit and vegetables, and any other supplies Mrs. Boone needed. When they left, they took back the fresh butter and cheese.

Daniel and his mother spent six summers this way. Later, he would remember these months as the best times of his life. Except for bringing in the cows and putting the cheese and butter in the spring, Daniel was free all day. He did some hunting with his bow and arrow, but mostly he hunted with a special weapon he made himself.

Daniel had pulled a young sapling, roots and all, from the soil. He stripped the bark from it, and tore off every branch. What he had left was a thin club with a round knob of roots at one end.

He practiced throwing it, like a tomahawk, at trees and rocks. Once Daniel's aim was close to perfect, he took his weapon and went hunting.

At first, he missed most of his moving targets. But Daniel kept at it. Soon he was using his club so well that he could hit rabbits and squirrels from as far away as ten yards.

For Daniel's twelfth birthday, his father gave him his first rifle. This was an important and proud moment for Daniel. It meant his parents thought of him as a young man, ready to accept a big responsibility.

"Daniel," his father said in a serious voice, "you've learned many things about living in this frontier. Now it's time you learned to use this rifle. I trust you'll always remember it's a tool—and should be used like one."

And then he smiled and presented Daniel with his birthday gift. "That rifle," Daniel remembered, "was the best gift anyone ever gave me." From that day on, Daniel was the family's number-one hunter. When there was a need for fresh meat, Mrs. Boone would send Daniel out for it. He never failed to come back with enough for everybody.

Daniel was such a sure shot and such a clever woodsman that his mother didn't worry about his safety. But one summer evening, when Daniel was thirteen, he didn't bring home the cows for milking. At first, Mrs. Boone just shook her head. She was certain she would see her son by bedtime. So she brought in the cows herself.

When Daniel still wasn't back the next morning, Mrs. Boone did begin to worry. Maybe he fell and broke a leg, she thought. Maybe he tangled with a wildcat. Maybe he met some unfriendly Indians. Something *had* to be wrong!

Mrs. Boone walked back to the farm and told her husband. Mr. Boone quickly put together a search party. For two days they looked for Daniel. They couldn't find a trace of him. Mr. Boone knew his son could move through the forest like a shadow and without leaving a trail—but right now he wished that Daniel wasn't quite *so* good at it!

At last, four days after the boy had disappeared, the searchers saw a wisp of smoke in the distance. It took them until nightfall to reach the source of it. What they found was a bark shelter, like the ones the Indians put up. Inside, sitting on a bearskin, was Daniel. He was roasting a chunk of bear meat over a fire, and smiling. The rest of the bear meat was cut up and hanging on tree branches outside the shelter.

"Were you lost?" Mr. Boone asked his son.

"Lost?" Daniel repeated, grinning. "No, sir. We're on the south side of Neversink Mountain. And maybe nine miles from the cow pasture."

"Why are you here?" Mr. Boone wanted to know. "Your mother has been sick with worry."

Daniel looked unhappy. "I'm sorry I gave her cause for worry," he said. "I got to tracking this bear. Well, he kept going, so I kept going. My mind was set on bringing him back. I think she'll be pleased to see all this meat."

"I think she'll be more pleased to see you!" Mr. Boone said.

And she was.

By the time he was in his early teens, Daniel was known far and wide as the finest shot and woodsman in Pennsylvania. The outdoors was his school, and he had no other. In fact, it wasn't until he was fourteen that Daniel learned to read and write. His teacher was his brother Samuel's bride. She did the best she could, but Daniel was not a very willing pupil.

Then the boy's Uncle John, who was a local teacher, took on the job. But he wasn't any more successful. Daniel couldn't bear to sit indoors, and he hated making those squiggly little letters with a quill pen. It was John Boone's turn to give up. He told Daniel's father that the boy was hopeless as a student.

Squire Boone shrugged his shoulders. "Let the others do the spelling," he said. "Daniel will do the hunting."

In 1750, when Daniel was fifteen, the Boones decided it was time to move on. With so many settlers pouring into Pennsylvania, Squire Boone was beginning to feel crowded. Many of the forests were being cut down to make way for new farm land, and the wild animals were being wiped out by hunters.

The Boones sold everything that couldn't be fitted onto a wagon and headed for Virginia. They all settled in western Virginia, except for Daniel. He and Henry Miller, who had been working for Mr. Boone, kept right on going. They went hunting and trapping, traveling as far as western North Carolina. When they had as many fur skins as they could carry, they headed home.

The stories they told of the beautiful mountains, the clear and sparkling streams, the rich soil, and the plentiful wild game—all this got the Boones packing and moving again. They reached western North Carolina and settled there for good. But not Daniel. Now that he had a taste of the real wilderness, he wanted to keep moving.

Daniel Boone's fame as a frontiersman grew quickly. In 1754, when he was almost twenty, the French and Indian War broke out. In it, English and colonial troops fought against Indians and French soldiers. Daniel joined the North Carolina Militia. His knowledge of the woods and Indian ways saved his life many times. It also saved many of his companions, British soldiers and colonial volunteers.

After the war, Daniel married Rebecca Bryan. They built a home in Sugartree Creek, North Carolina, cleared some land for farming, and began to raise a family. But Daniel wasn't done with wandering. He continued to hunt and trap and explore the wilderness. He went off to fight in the Cherokee War in 1758. Two years after that he became one of the first frontiersmen to reach Tennessee.

In 1765, Daniel went as far south as Florida. He made the journey just to see more of what was "out there." Then, in 1767, he set foot in Kentucky for the first time. This was to become his home for many years.

Daniel loved the wilderness. He roamed through the forests and across the grassy fields. He hunted deer and buffalo. Nobody knew this uncharted territory better than Daniel Boone.

Then, in 1775, a large company bought twenty million acres of this rich land from the Cherokee Indians. The company owners planned to sell parcels of land to settlers from the colonies. But first they needed someone to open a trail into the territory and to start a settlement there.

The man they chose for the job was Daniel. They couldn't have picked a better one. He knew where the spring rains turned the soil to swamp. He knew where the land was too rocky for farming. And he also knew where good farming and hunting lands were.

Daniel knew of one very special spot. It was an open plain near a bend on the south bank of the Kentucky River. All around stood giant sycamore trees. And there was a salt lick nearby, at the mouth of Otter Creek. Deer and buffalo liked the salt there, so the hunting was ideal. This was the spot Daniel chose for the settlement.

In March 1775, Daniel led a party of thirty settlers into the Kentucky territory. It took them weeks to reach Otter Creek, two hundred-fifty miles from their starting place. The party wanted to turn back several times, but, urged on by Daniel's strength and spirit, they kept going.

Cutting a road through the wild and beautiful land was hard work. The pioneers had to axe their way through the forests. Some days the hardy group covered a good distance. Other days the going was tough. There were deep, rocky ravines to bridge. Huge trees that took hours to bring down. Rainy weather that slowed their progress to a crawl.

There were Indians to worry about, too. Daniel could always sense when danger was nearby. Thanks to his leadership, they were able to drive off a party of hostile Shawnee Indians, losing only two of their group. And a number of other times Daniel kept the pioneers quiet and hidden, while unfriendly Indians passed by.

They finally reached Otter Creek on the evening of April 1. Behind them stretched a ribbon of winding trail that came to be known as Wilderness Road. It was a rough trail, just wide enough for wagons to ride over. But in the years to come, thousands of wagons would follow Daniel's trail. It was the beginning of the long road to the West.

The settlement was built on the beautiful and special place that Daniel had chosen. The first building was a fort, named Fort Boone in honor of their leader. Soon a number of cabins were built, fields were cleared and planted, and families began to settle there. A town had come to life in the wilderness. And again Daniel was honored when the town was named Boonesboro.

Daniel and Rebecca had ten children. Daniel taught the boys to hunt and shoot, but it was Rebecca who raised the family, and took care of their farm. Daniel was away from home for months at a time.

While he was away, he might be fighting the Indians in Kentucky, or living in a Shawnee camp as the adopted son of Chief Blackfish. He might be leading parties of settlers through unmapped forests, hills, and plains. Or he might be off on his own, hunting, trapping—blazing new trails in the endless wilderness of the young nation. The itch to be out there, in a world known only to the Indians, was part of Daniel to the end of his life.

When he died, on September 26, 1820, Daniel
had become a legend. He was eighty-six years old,
and had spent almost every one of those years
exploring the wilderness. More than anyone else
in American history, Daniel Boone is remembered
and admired as the greatest frontiersman of all.